'Tis an old tale, and often told; But did my fate and wish agree, Ne'er had been read, in story old, Of maiden true betray'd for gold, That loved, or was avenged, like me!

-Sir Walter Scott

Ladies, do not get mad: get even!

1

Sandy Daley

"Whose *Vagina* Is It, Really *?*"

By

Sandy Daley

THE POWER OF THE P!

The power of the vagina, or the power of the P, as many would call it, is a real, viable, and attainable thing. He who holds the key to the vagina maintains the control. Many would say that the world is about two things: power and control.

Control your vagina and maintain your power. But does it belong to you? Is there ever a time when your vagina belongs to you and you alone -besides the times when you are using the bathroom? Ever wonder why it is in such high demand by everyone?

Praise for Sandy's work and the book:

"Whose Vagina Is It, Really?"

"Sandy's anecdotes and articles are always refreshing and entertaining. Her writing always touches me in some way because she talks about what women are experiencing in their relationships. Keep up the good work, Sandy."

-Trudy-Ann Ewan, Motivational Speaker

"Talented actress Sandy Daley has a strong passion for writing and is not afraid to delve into issues concerning family, women, love, love lost, and relationships- some of which have impacted her own life as a single mother of two kids. Don't be deceived by the title; her book is funny, elegant, informative, educational yet entertaining, and gives a bird's-eye view into the psyche of women. This enlightening book is her story and the story of many women. It is a must read for men wanting to understand the puzzling women in their life."

- Anthony Turner, Media Marketer

"Extraordinarily gripping read, love your angle! When you smile, the world smiles back at you. Keep on smiling Sandy."

-Shareen Earle Greaves, Behavioural Specialist

The road to self-actualization begins when one realizes that one's own path has been blocked and one's progress in life will depend on the choices one makes, along with one's determination to succeed, whatever the cost. In *"Whose Vagina Is It, Really?"*, Sandy Daley shares her personal stories and experiences, which have redefined her path towards life in a way that allows her to make those choices that only she can, and will make.

"Whose Vagina Is It, Really?" started out as a "closet experience" where her journals became a mirror and a personal escape to understand her own life, set new goals, and crash the male-dominated barriers that placed limits on sexual and emotional freedoms for women. Sharing her journal with friends and colleagues, Sandy realized that her own story is woven into the fabric of the daily life of women she meets.

This realization leads to the fulfillment of *"Whose Vagina Is It, Really?"* Funny, sensitive, controversial, and direct, *"Whose Vagina Is It, Really?"* offers suggestions for women who are at their wits' end regarding their relationships, family, and personal lives. This book allows women the opportunity to make their own choices, based on where they may be at that moment in their lives.

-Pablo Assab, ESPN staff writer

"Sandy says what I wish I could say. I wish I had the guts to say what she says. When I read her articles, I feel as if she is speaking to me. Way to go, girl!"

-Antoniette Facey, Social worker

"Wow, girl, this is popping...never thought of that...ur rite!! Lol."

– Melissa Blessed Gayle

"Reading this book made me learn more about women than I had known before. Sandy says it like it is and does not sugarcoat anything. Way to go, Sandy!"

-Asim Khan, York University student

"Men do not like to admit to even momentary imperfection. My husband forgot the code to turn off the alarm. When the police came, he wouldn't admit he'd forgotten the code...he turned himself in."

-RITA RUDNER

Dedication

To my very brave children, Shane and Warren. You have both made me very proud; hopefully I can reciprocate. To Auntie Merlene, Auntie P and Sis Norma, (you all deserve your own sitcom).

To my mom especially, thank you for showing me how strong a woman can *really* be. You are both mother and *father* to Trecia, Andre, and I.

To all the ladies and gentlemen that I met along the way; without you, this book could never have been done. Thanks for sharing- although some of you did not even know that you were.

Sandy Daley

"Men are simple things. They can survive a whole weekend with only three things: beer, boxer shorts and batteries for the remote control."

-DIANA JORDAN.

Contents

Foreword

"Whose Vagina Is It, Really?" — the ideal teaching tool for the girls, but the instructive eye-opener for men! Everybody requires enduring behavioral interdependence, repeated interactions, emotional attachment, and need fulfillment. Undoubtedly, intimate relationships play a central role in the overall human experience. Humans have a universal need which is satisfied when intimate relationships are formed with another human being.

However, intimate relationships consist of the people that we are attracted to, whom we like and love, romantic and sexual relationships, and those who we marry and provide with emotional and personal support. With the divorce rate in America and other countries estimated at over 50 percent for the past ten years, an increasing number of people are finding it affordable and less nerve-racking to be engaged in noncommittal intimate relationships. While money and other resources are always a major spotlight in most relationships, the woman's body, especially the vagina, continues to be the focal point of the relationships.

For most women, their vagina is their prized possession, power, and bargaining chip. On the other hand, it is the opinion of most men that a woman's vagina is for them to keep and care for as long as they are paying the bills and providing food and shelter.

As the vagina fights between men and woman continue, one of the most prolific and modern-day writers, Sandy Daley, has put forward some solutions in *"Whose Vagina Is It, Really?"* in her own unique and hilarious style. Sandy encourages women to keep the power, while demanding more respect and understanding from men.

Sandy skillfully ignores the idiom, "He who pays the piper calls the tune." She comments that men may have the money and are paying bills, but they should not dictate the terms of the relationship. The writer urges women to "Love yourself before anyone else; but love him wholeheartedly as well if you have chosen him. Oftentimes we become nags and don't support our men. If you want him and he is worth it and he is the One, then love him the right way."

"Whose Vagina Is It, Really?" is the ideal teaching tool for the girls, but the instructive eye-opener for men. Funny, but conscious writings.

-Patrick Maitland, publisher, *Street Hype* newspaper

Introduction

They say that good things sometimes are the result of a bad situation, and this book is a true testament to that statement. I met a man whom I thought was "the one". I ran to my girlfriends- specifically my hairdresser/girlfriend J- boasted about him loudly, and thought that I had found true love. Boy was I ever wrong! Not only did he turn out to be the biggest womanizer that I have ever met, but a major jerk as well. And he was an "almost pastor" — and that's another thing: how could you be an "almost pastor"? It's either you are a pastor or not, right? He sat in the front of the pew in the church when Sundays rolled around, with the mind of a major pervert behind closed doors.

The man brought up things in bed that I have never thought about, things that should never be repeated, but use your imagination. So here I was, now dealing with not only a womanizer, but I was also messing with the Church and God. I ran with my tail between my legs, praying each day that the Lord would forgive me for my transgressions. I had always seen myself as a possible "Preacher's wife", with all the perks that come along with the title. However, I did not think that God would approve of how I would have ended up in that stately position. Fire and brimstone, and of course my

Pentecostal upbringing, won over my lust and desires. I desperately tried to put this man, whom I thought was going to be my husband, out of my head.

To ease my pain, I threw myself into my work, trying to ease the pain without turning to alcohol. And a funny thing happened along the way: the more I wrote, the better I felt. Women and men also took notice of what I had to say in my weekly column in Streethype Newspaper, and they related to my thoughts and honesty. They laughed, cried, and went along with me as I tried to restore myself and heal my broken heart.

Then months later, after no contact whatsoever, this same "almost pastor" called me out of the blue one night and asked, "So is it still mine Sandy?" He went on to say, "Hopefully you have not been giving my pussy away to anyone?" I could not believe my ears! "The nerve of him," I thought to myself. Hence, "Whose Vagina Is It, Really?" was born, and a whole can of worms was opened up. Women understood my question and men could not believe that I, a woman, had the balls to ask such a question. Every event or function that I attended, "So whose is it really Sandy?" was the question that was asked of me by almost every man who had heard rumors about my upcoming book. Normal conversations flew out the window!

So for that, I thank my Mr. Wonderful for allowing me to make lemonade out of lemons and to, more importantly, bring laughter, joy, and a lot of insight to other women. For the other women in your makeshift Western- like harem, I say; thank you as well. Still yet, I am hopeful for everlasting love, as one bad apple does not spoil the bunch.

Over the year, I spoke to both men and women (unbeknownst to many of them), desperately seeking the answers that I needed as to why men act the way they do. I wanted to learn from my mistakes as well. I desired no further stupid moves in my future love endeavors. The answers that I sought however, did not come from others, but instead came to me from my very own words. So, in this book, you will see not only my stories and experiences as I exhaled each week with my column, but also case studies of other women as well. This book is unscripted and comes from a very real place.

Boy, did I learn a lot! I learned that women are still viewed as mainly objects of desire and that our lives are never one dimensional. We love our men and our families with no boundaries at all. I also learned that we make a lot of mistakes when it comes to our guys and how we deal with them. When a man chooses a woman, it is a big deal for him, as men have so many women to choose from, because of the ratio of men to women.

Our men feel let down however, especially after they have chosen us as their "wives" and many, "do not trust us to care emotionally for them." My heart was pulled by its strings while listening to men over the year. I began to truly understand their position for the very first time. Most men do not set out to cheat on you when they get with you; they want to stay and be with only *you*. You, however, need to help them along and, yes, use your vagina to make things work for you at home.

Through self-examination, lots of research, and a lot of listening, *"Whose Vagina Is It, Really?"* will allow you to get to the heart of the matter. Men and women are to be held accountable for what happens in a relationship, and *"Whose Vagina Is It, Really?"* is a guide of sorts to help you along the way. But it is still up to you to implement these suggestions and use my, and other people's experiences to help you in your own life.

With each story, you will be able to see yourself and make the decision as to what is best for *you* and *you* alone. And if you wish to be single for the rest of your life, and swing from the chandeliers with different men every other night- with protection of course- then the choice should be yours. If you wish to find that perfect mate and settle down, the choice is still yours. The vagina belongs to you! Do what you want with it! God is not going to take it back for over- or -under usage.

Note: All the names in this book have been changed, in order to

protect the identity of the people mentioned.

Let's take it from the beginning!

The article that started it all!

PICK TILL SHE PICK CRAP?

As the New Year rolled around and the past year became nothing but a distant memory, I stared at the man beside me in the huge king-size bed with posters on the ceiling in Ohio and wondered, "Am I finally going to have a man in my life that I do not emotionally kill?" I mean, he was a gorgeous specimen of a man; tall, dark, handsome, smart, intelligent, and ambitious. He was also very funny; all the qualities that I liked in a man. Of course, I had also tested out the goods — if you know what I mean — and this man was a definite keeper with a capital K. I don't care what us girls say, "Size does matter!" Newsflash to all the guys, it does!

He was a definite plus, and I could see myself growing old with him, but as all women know, if the man does not know what he has in front of him, it will never, ever work! I am baffled, as most of my friends and especially my mother are, as to why I am still single. I cannot count the number of times my mother has sat in our family dining room, looked me seriously in the eye, and asked, "Sandy, are you sure that you are not a lesbian? Why don't you have a man? Do you want to die alone?" I figured that she must know a thing or two; she is sixty years old and has been single for almost twenty years. I cannot say that I have not had my chances to become a wife or a significant partner to a few good men, but for some reason it has never gotten to that final stage. Some of the times I honestly think that I messed up my own chances of marriage.

There was the ambitious lawyer boyfriend in Atlanta, who loved me dearly and only begged me to, "lie in the bed with me Sandy, and hug me." At that time of my life it was all about my career, and lying in bed with him in the middle of the day seemed like such a waste of my valuable time. I do miss him sometimes though, as he taught me to "smell the roses and relax sometimes". Then there was the personal trainer who begged me to be his "second wife", as he put it. He was married already, of course, but just wanted to take care of me. Of course, I said, "Thanks, but no thanks." I mean, geez, why would I want to be with a married man, no matter how much money a month he wanted to give me for my bills? The last time he offered, he was had raised his amount to $500 per month. Still, I said, "thanks, but no thanks!"Needless to say, after my flat-out no, he refused to continue training me. "I will not make you any sexier for any other man," he said. Men! Such babies! I still care for him deeply though, as he at least knew how to take care of a woman. He was from the Middle East, and having two or three wives is okay he says, as long as the man was able to support all of them.

Then there was the businessman from Georgia who offered me a Visa to the United States, as long I became his "woman". I mean, he was truly nice and all-at first-, but began acting kind of crazy: threatening me, crying on the phone, and e-mailing me every two seconds, when I refused his advances. I like a man that shows me that he truly cares, but I don't like a nut job, Visa or no Visa! I turned him down of course, and ran from the stronghold that he tried to have placed on me. To this day, I still envision him walking around, mumbling to himself, somewhere in the suburbs of Georgia. My girlfriend says that I must have "laid" it on him too good and so he was a little bit whipped. I'll run with that; my stuff is good, or so I have been told!

Trust me, friends, the life of a single girl is fulfilling and interesting, to say the least, but with no one to share it with, at times it seems meaningless. I keep thinking that I am too picky and set in my ways, so therefore I am single and without an official man by my side. I truly do have high hopes for this sexy brother and myself in Ohio, and like most women with a new love, I am intrigued by him. Occasionally, we do have our moments of anger and miscommunication, but his demeanor, self-confidence, and ability to stay toe to toe with me is at times quite humorous.

He says that I "wear him out", but in my opinion he should consider himself very lucky that he is even getting the chance. "Do you know how many men would die to get worn out by me?" I asked him jokingly. I have to put him in his place sometimes of course. Women need to know their worth, and I know mine! I have come to the conclusion after pondering this issue intently over the last few weeks that I am not the one choosing a partner for me. Those past relationships did not work because they were not supposed to.

The higher power up above, I believe, knows who is good for me and whom I am good for. I am getting prepared for "the one", my Mr. Wonderful. As women, we need to trust the Universe, and not settle for anything but the best. We often tend to look at our age, as my mother does, as a sign that it is time to find that perfect man and settle down, no matter what is wrong in our relationships. Being emotional creatures, our tendency is to make decisions based on feelings, and often times desperation, as our age increases.

Being forty and single is not a badge that I wear with *honor*, but it is a true testament that I, Ms. Sandy Daley, am still hopeful that my Prince Charming will ride along on a white horse, with good credit and white teeth of course. He will whisk me up, kiss me squarely on my lips, and whisper in my ear, "Where have you been all my life?" I wonder if Mr. Ohio knows how to ride a horse?

From my weekly column, "Real Talk with Sandy"

The Break-up

Needless to say, my relationship with Mr. Ohio, my Mr. Wonderful did not last! It however, served as an inspiration for this book. Not because I was saddened and heartbroken at its failure, but because it taught me so much, gave me so much, and finally made me aware of things that I had been doing wrong in my search for love.

There is no bitterness at all towards my "Mr. Wonderful" – as I like to call him- just the utmost of gratitude. His actions have truly allowed me to shine, and have enabled me to share so much to the world. No two people are the same, but everyone should set their own boundaries, similar to what I have done, and I share with you, in the following pages.

Enjoy!

*The Choice*_____

The following are some of *my* personal do's and don'ts that I now live by. Over the years, I have set many rules, broken many, but there are some that will never change. Case studies of wonderful women are also intertwined throughout, to help highlight the issues as I see fit. Maybe you can use all, or some, or none of the suggestions if you wish.

The choice is yours to make.

*Anita*_____

"Nature intended women to be our slaves. They are our property."

—Napoleon Bonaparte

The stand-by-your-man type of woman. Hails from the Midwest! They say that they make good wives! Maybe I need to visit!

To say that Anita is the perfect wife would be an understatement. She has never worked since the children were born, and her goal in life is to keep her family intact. She cooks, cleans, does the groceries, takes care of the bills, looks after the children, and is the glue that keeps her family together. Her husband John is a systems analyst with the government and is the primary breadwinner in the family. He is never home most nights, goes away on extended holidays on his own, and never ever takes Anita out on dates.

Her house is paid for, her children attend great schools, there is money in the bank, food on the table, credit cards in her wallet—but she is not happy. She knows that something is wrong because there is no intimacy in the marriage. Her husband makes no sexual advances towards her anymore, and she wonders if he is cheating. "Do you not find me attractive anymore John?" she asks. "We have not made love in five months, and you do not seem worried about that. Why don't you come to bed at night and not sleep in the couch? John, please talk to me!" But there is never a response. The most that she has ever gotten from him is, "Anita, a lot of women would kill to be in your shoes. You have a beautiful home, money in your pocket, and food on the table, and you have never had to work for any of these things. What is your problem? Just leave well enough alone!"

Maybe she was crazy, she thought. Maybe she wanted too much out of life. What *is* wrong with her? She must stop nagging her husband for affection and care as she has a lot in life, more than a lot of other women. So what if he is cheating with someone else? At least he comes home! "Get it together Anita," she rationalizes. "Play your role as a good wife and leave the man alone!"

Chapter #1_____

Do:

You come first at all times (even if he is your husband).

It is a fact that most women put others before themselves. It is a rare thing to see a woman who puts herself before others without her feeling guilty, or society calling her selfish or an unfit mother. Have you ever seen that woman, a businesswoman most times, running around, having that kid on her hip or in her office, while she is on the phone doing fifty million things at once? She kills herself trying to please everyone and at the end of the day, is made to feel like a bad mother and wife because she wants—God forbid— a "career". The funny thing is, that husband of hers has no qualms about cheating on her with his secretary or going off with his buddies golfing or to soccer practice. Their swings are off, their soccer outfits don't fit anymore, and there is no hope in hell that they will ever play competitively again; but still yet they go. Her "career" takes a backseat to everything else around her, and she never accomplishes all that she could have.

In regards to the children, what I have learnt, and what has been my personal experience, is that children grow up. They will leave you when they are good and ready, not when you are ready for them to go. They too, want their own lives. You might get a call from the kids one day a week when they are adults; if you are lucky. Take the time to take that Course that you have always wanted to, go for that promotion that you want and take that stripping class that's always intrigued you. Also, spend time by yourself and with your girlfriends. Live a little. This not only allows you the freedom to have your own identity, but it also cushions the blows that come later on in life when the kids leave the nest or your husband finds himself going through a midlife crisis. Who knows? He might want to *bang* a twenty-year-old woman, with bigger, perkier boobs than yours, who of course also an ass that you are able to place your drink on, with ease. The "chair butt girl", is what I call her! Remember when you had one of those?

So what if they consider you selfish because you went on that Mediterranean cruise with your girls' and left the family behind? So what if you are now enrolling in the new striptease class down the street, and getting your freak on with the girls? Whose life is it really, yours or someone else's? When God created you, you were born alone (even twins have to come out one at a time). Act like an individual and get your own life.

Sandy Daley

"Men who don't understand women fall into two groups:
Bachelors and Husbands."
-JACQUES LANGUIRAND

DEIDRA

"One of the reasons I don't see eye to eye with women's lib is that women have it all on a plate if only they knew it. They don't have to be pretty either."

-Charlotte Rampling

The girl with no Valentines! The Buckeye girl: Cincinnati never looked so good!

If there were three words to describe Deidra, they would be "average," "average," and "average" again! She will never be seen in anything too skimpy or revealing, and her wardrobe is made up of scarves, turtlenecks (even for the summer), and long skirts that go way below her knees. At twenty-eight years old and reasonably attractive, you would think that her social calendar would be filled with dates for each week. Yet her Christian upbringing, which dictates her life social life, demands that she does not date. According to the members of the congregation in the Church, the Lord will send her a husband whom she will grow to love, even without her really getting to know him.

So a Valentine's night is similar to all the other nights; spent at home all by herself. "Why aren't you on a date tonight?" her friend Jessica asked her while she was on the phone. "Deidra, no man is going to find you all cooped up in the house," she said. "I know that Peter the cable guy asked you out tonight and you told him no. Why, when you have no one to go with and you are all alone?" Jessica asked.

Deidra had no answer to Jessica's queries because there was none. Does she not deserve love, or a partner, or even just a date? Peter was an attractive man, and even though he might not be "the one," he would have been a fun date, as he was witty and intelligent. Yes, his beard was a little too thick for her liking and his pants a little too tight around the bum area, but so what? He was still a good catch. What really was her issue? Was Christianity so entrenched in her psyche that she could not date anyone, as the church had instructed? Not God, but the church members!

Next year, she rationalizes; she will go on a date with someone on Valentine's night, even if he is not Mr. Right. At least it will be better than being alone on Valentine's night. She does not even care what little ol' nosey Ms. Grace, who sits in the front pew, would say! "To hell with her," she thought. "Ms. Grace already has her husband. Even if he was dried up like an old prune!"

*Chapter #2*_____

Do:

Date lots of men (think of your dating pool as a basketball team). This does not mean that I want to see you on an episode of Maury asking, "Who's your baby daddy?"

When it comes to dating, women have it all wrong and totally backwards. The thing with us girls is that most of the time, intimacy means that we fall in love as soon as we have given a man a "piece", as we sometimes call it. We are programmed to think that we are sluts if we are seeing more than one man at a time.

A man however, is given a pat on the back for being a "man" when he has lots of women. Your new strategy in this whole dating game is to date lots of men, to help you figure out who is your *right* partner. Now, be careful here, as you really don't want to sleep with every man, but you should find a way to *see* lots of men at the same time. You are really searching for your match.

My brother suggested that I, and other women, should, "think of your dating pool as a basketball team Sandy, with forwards and defensive players, and players who sometimes stay on the bench." I liked his reasoning, and so I ran with it. Let's say there is one guy that you like a lot. He is your forward. He is the one that you want, but the trick is not to make him feel *too* special, as not only will he become complacent but, who knows, someone else might step up and try to take his spot. Have you ever seen that pretty girl with a good job, nice body, and intelligent wit about her? She constantly tells you her man's reluctance to really commit to her, even though she sleeps with no one else, and has no other man around her. She has settled with this nonchalant behavior from her man.

Don't settle for that half-assed behavior from *your* man. Unless you make it known that you are seeing other men and that you have other prospects, you will be seen as nothing but an easy lay that needs no commitment. Now if you *don't* really want to have commitment from this man, then of course that is all fine. Continue doing what you are doing. If you decide to make a go at it and you want a relationship, make it known and see your man's reaction. If he is flippant and does not seem to care one way or the other if another man is putting his hands on you, and loving you, do yourself a favor and move on. He only wants sex from you. If that is *not* what you want, why stay and waste your time and energies on someone who does not want you that much?

Go on to the next man and do not think twice about it. If your neighbor sees you with Tom one day and Dick the other day, who cares? Look her straight in the eye and ask her, "By any chance do you know of a man that could fit into my basketball group?" The backlash that you will receive is nothing compared to the heartache that you will have over the next few years if you choose the wrong person, and did not *date* to find your true partner. Men do it all the time. You should as well!

"Aggression is part of the masculine design, we are hardwired for it.... Little girls do not invent games where large numbers of people die, where bloodshed is a prerequisite for having fun. Hockey, for example, was not a feminine creation. Nor was boxing. A boy wants to attack something -- and so does a man, even if it's only a little white ball on a tee."

JOHN ELDREDGE, *WILD AT HEART*

*Courtney-Ann*_____

"Guys are like dogs. They keep coming back. Ladies are like cats. Yell at a cat one time…they're gone."

- Lenny Bruce

The girl with the stalker ex-boyfriend! Bright lights, big city: What happens in Vegas stays in Vegas. So did Courtney-Ann!

Courtney- Ann was at her wits' end. What in God's name was she going to do now and who was going to help her? If she had known that Jason would turn out to be such a menace, a problem to her, she would never have accepted his phone number or gotten to know him; much less have an intimate relationship with the man. After months of dating, and many arguments in between, she had decided to terminate her relationship with him, but unfortunately he did not like the idea.

He had threatened her on countless occasions with bodily harm if she ever slept with another man. Not only had he broken into her e-mails, as his job as an IT professional enabled him to figure out codes and Internet programs, but he was also sending her harassing e-mails and making phone calls to anyone who would listen to him. "My gosh," she thought. "My loving must be something else." This situation was confusing to her and she was at a loss of how to handle it. The fact was that they were not suited for each other. He was an introvert with no one to call a friend besides his computers and software devices, while she, on the other hand, was vivacious and full of life. Her personality was vibrant, intoxicating, and he wanted to latch onto her at any cost. It was obvious to her that they did not make a good match, but to him, she seemed to be his lifeline to the world.

In his mind, if he controlled her life, her every move, her desires, she would eventually love him, the way he needed to be loved by someone; anyone. Unfortunately for him, Courtney-Ann was a free spirit. She was an independent woman who had no desires to be controlled, and fought tooth and nail to maintain the control in her own life. No matter what threats or coercion tactics Jason tried, Courtney-Ann fought him. "Let him bring it," she thought. "If he wants a fight, then a fight is what he will get." "First things first though," she thought. "The police must be called to at least notify them of this fool." If only she had spent the time to get to know Jason fully, she would never have become the victim of a stalker. Her Facebook and Twitter accounts were never the same again. Aww…the era of the Internet. The good must come with the bad, of course!

*Chapter #3*_____

Do:

If the kids don't like him, investigate your Mr. Wonderful discreetly. You might have a stalker on your hands!

This is a very, very tricky subject — kids and the new man. Here is the scenario: you have met your Mr. Wonderful, who rocks your world, buys you flowers, and pays you the attention that you like. The only problem is that the kids keep telling you, "Mommy, Donovan is weird and gives me a creepy feeling."

If you are a single mother with a teenage daughter, you pay attention right away to every statement that she makes. No man is worth damaging your relationship with your child, and you should never allow any man to come between you and your children. You will find another man, and your child, especially a daughter, will never forgive you if she opens up herself to you and you don't listen. There are many women out there — many lonely women, I might add — who are desperate for love and will take it any which way, shape, or form in which it is given to them.

They might be in their thirties, still attractive, and finding the pool of pickings getting shallower, and they are desperate to take anything that comes their way. All your friends might be married or in a relationship except you, and you are beginning to doubt yourself. Don't! Do you really know your Mr. Wonderful? When we meet a man, most times we are so focused on his charm, good looks and his big bank account. We keep dreaming about this gorgeous specimen of a man who will be the father of our children.

We push aside everything else that comes our way about this man, even if it is staring us in the face. "Girl, so what if he does not ever answer his phone during the night when I call, or if he always freaks out for nothing while we are in a discussion?" is what we often say to our girlfriends while we gush over our Mr. Wonderful. The only thing that we forget is that most people hide their true personalities from us, masking who they really are until we have gotten to like them and are drawn into their world.

By then it is difficult to break free. The first six to eight months of any friendship or relationship is based on superficial feelings, created by superficial character traits. You have to take your time to really get to know a man, any man. Find out who this person really is. You do not want to open up your heart and your home to someone who will not respect, love, or care for you the way you should be cared for.

Even worse, do you know how many crazy people are running around in this world? Can you imagine, and unfortunately I can attest to this, getting involved with someone, letting them into your life, only to find out a year later that they are mentally unstable, and should not be allowed anywhere near common-sense folks?

Time—no matter your age, status in life, how much money you have in the bank, or how pretty or desirable you are—is your best friend; use it wisely. A man will show you only what he wants to show you in the beginning (and of course we all know what his first objective is). It's important to get to *know* him deeper than simply listening to him tell you what you want to hear- just so that he can get into your pants.

One encounter could result in your life being ruined in many ways, and this ladies, is no joke. So take the time to get to know him, and if you can't figure him out by yourself during those first few months, hire someone to do so. Also, check Google, Facebook and MySpace for any information on this man. The Internet, which can be a source of many bad things, can also work in your favor. Do you know that many employers these days do not even look at your resumes or your references, but first turn to the Internet to find out about their possible employee?

Although the information that is out there might be incorrect, at least you can gain a sense of who it is that you are dealing with. If it is good for your boss and big businesses, why shouldn't it be good for you? Then, if you find out something that is not showing your tall, dark, and handsome in a favorable light, be as honest as possible and ask your Mr. Wonderful about what you have learned. Of course, don't approach the topic without another person there beside you. Why take a chance and have him flip out on you at the thought of you doing a background check on him? In the long run, he will see the wisdom of your ways, and this will demonstrate to him that you value your safety and respect your surroundings. If he has a problem with this and is not willing to be upfront with you, then leave. No use wasting your time, and there might be some truth to what is out there if he is not willing to meet you halfway.

And don't forget to listen, listen, and then listen some more to what your children think, if they know him that is. It is often best that they are left out of the picture entirely when you are dating, so as not to get them emotionally involved in your love life. When things are very serious, then they should be introduced to your mate. Treat your children like rare expensive meat-not everyone gets to indulge.

My own children, to use an example from my own life, have always picked up on things that I did not notice. One man that I dated a few years back always walked with a limp and had a major cleft at the bottom of his chin. I, of course, overlooked these physical shortcomings, but my children would actually make jokes in front of me about my new man. "Mom, don't you notice that Donovan walks funny and has a weird look in his eyes?"We had been dating for a very long time and so he had been introduced to my boys.

Of course, my first reaction to the children was to dismiss them from my sight for being "rude and disrespectful" to an adult. In my opinion, he had always been kind to them. One day however, I decided to take matters into my own hands and asked Donovan if there was something that he needed to tell me about his limp and his cleft.

Reluctantly, he admitted that a year prior, while going through his divorce -which was now almost final, as he had been fully separated when we first met and had shown me separation papers to prove it- had decided that life was not worth living. He had jumped off the third-story building where he lived to "end it all".

Shocked and horrified, I comforted Donovan and assured him that it was going to be okay, as I was his friend and was happy that nothing worse had happened to him. Call me wicked, but I broke up with Donovan a week later, using the façade that "I wanted to concentrate on my work and had no time for a relationship." I assured him that he was a great guy, and of course it is "my loss". Of course, the real reason was that I thought that he was not a stable individual if he was willing to attempt suicide. Why would I want that type of personality around me, as well as around my children?

The flip side to it was that to me, he was kind of a coward to jump from the third floor, as obviously he must have known that he would not die. In my mind he was just looking for sympathy and attention. A coward and unstable! My two pet peeves! I did say to call me wicked, did I not? So listen to your children as I finally did to mine. Who knows, Donovan might have pushed *me* instead over the fourth-floor balcony the next time that he wanted to "end it all". I would not only end up with a cleft and a limp, but also at least a broken arm. I heard through the grapevine recently that he had gotten remarried to another beautiful woman who was also a nurse. Deep within my heart I wished him well; but felt no pangs of jealously. I hope they live in a bungalow for her sake! Hopefully her nursing skills will not have to be too handy at home. Okay, I know, that was mean-spirited!

Remember, kids see what we cannot, as our judgment is clouded, and often-times we are blinded by a large penis or an even bigger bank account (and none of these will ever stand the test of time). Penises shrink in the pool, men lose their virility over time, and we are in a major recession, so you never know who will still be maintaining their wealth over time.

Sandy Daley

"What are the three words guaranteed to humiliate men everywhere? 'Hold my purse.'"

-FRANCOIS MORENCY

Marsha _____

"When I have one foot in the grave, I will tell the whole truth about women. I shall tell it, jump into my coffin, pull the lid over me, and say, 'Do what you like now. "

-Leo Tolstoy

Desperately Seeking Herself!

The hot Trinidadian mama: One of Trinidad and Tobago's finest!

Marsha, forty-five and still single, lit up a room when she walked in. Yes, her temper was too short, skirt too tight, lipstick too bright, and she was a few pounds overweight, but her personality was intoxicating. She still knew how to turn heads! Her divorce from Peter was now final, and she was beginning to feel as if she could not cope.

She had not thought about her own future while she had been married. Her only child Zachery, was the light of her life, but with him living miles away while at college, Marsha was often left all alone, preferring not to indulge too much in the party scene.

Her job as a manager for a clothing company was secure, although her financial portfolio could be a little healthier. Although she had never filed for bankruptcy, she was beginning to consider it. The situation was getting to be a little stressful because of all the years of raising a son by herself, and taking care of the bills. Her dating life was nonexistent. However, over the last few years, she had seriously attempted to find Mr. Right, and had failed miserably and given up.

Despite the failures, Marsha continued to work, pay her bills, and work out at the gym, while silently praying that Mr. Right would come waltzing through her door."You are never going to get that," said her friend Malcolm. "Just find a man who likes you, and even if you don't like him that much, you'll learn to love him. You will see how good it can be." Maybe Malcolm was right. "What the heck is going to happen to me now that I am all alone and Zachery is at school?" she asked herself. Marsha wished that she had listened to her inner voice and put something away for herself while she had been married to Peter. "I wonder if the Lord can send me a man now," she wondered. She needed help with the bills! Desperation was surely setting in!

*Chapter #4*_____

Do:

Money, money, money!

Keep some money for yourself (even if you have to open up an offshore account or keep money in your panty drawer. He will never look there!)

Nothing breaks up a relationship more often than money. This subject is a very touchy one, and many of your friends don't even know how to discuss money with their spouses or partners. Money drives a wedge between partners if not dealt with properly. The thing is, women usually make less money than men, and often times after a divorce, are thrown into poverty. Men, on the other hand, always seem to bounce back faster and land on their feet unscathed if there is a divorce.

That is why I would always suggest that a woman have a stash of dough just for herself, put away where no one knows about it — especially not her children. In case you do go through a divorce, you and your children will not be left stranded on the streets.

Okay, let's get this straight; I am not saying to take from your children's mouths or your husband's belly during marriage. However, there are a few ways that you can ensure that *just in case* you ever go through a divorce or separation, you are not thrown into a shelter. Living in your parents' basement for the rest of your life is also not a wonderful arrangement. There are many ways to skin a cat, and you can certainly save during the years without hurting the family.

One good way is to buy store-brand products while doing the grocery shopping, or even having a little home business of your own while doing your job as a stay-at-home mom. Okay, so you might feel a little funny skimming a little off the top from the grocery money, but think of it as sealing the deal in *you* making sure that you are not left in dire need if you ever go through a divorce. As a single woman, especially with children, it is even more important that you keep some money for yourself.

The life of a single gal is never easy, as all the bills are your responsibility. The cable bill, the car payment, the rent, and of course you have to eat and look presentable at the same time. With no one to share the bills with, life will not be easy, so you need to step up your game a bit. Get a life insurance policy, open a savings account, cut back on the hair and nail visits, and look at your financial life as a job. No one will care about your well-being but you, so therefore you must show some care about *your* own financial stability.

If you are married, open up an account somewhere your husband does not know about and won't suspect. How often have you seen that woman who lives with her husband for a number of years, and if she ever gets a divorce, she has no leg to stand on and nothing but a prayer by her side to make it? Don't be a statistic! Put aside some dough for yourself; more than likely, he is doing so too, without you even knowing about it.

Sandy Daley

"A genius is a man who can rewrap a new shirt and not have any pins left over."
-Dino Levi

SADE

"Women should have labels on their foreheads saying, 'Government Health Warning: women can seriously damage your brains, genitals, current account, confidence, razor blades, and good standing among your friends.' "

-Jeffrey Bernard

The hot body girl with no man! Philly baby-Philly cheesecake with extra cheese of course!

There has never been a time when Sade has really ever been alone. Getting dates was never a problem for her. Sade knew she had it going on, and she let everyone else know it as well.

Her work as a fitness instructor allowed her to meet lots of single men on a regular basis, and her social calendar was always full. She was up to almost 2,000 people as friends on her Facebook page, and had recently been warned that she could not accept anymore friends, or her account would be shut down. She now needed a fan page! But her dates all added up to nothing; they all had the same issue, which was why none of them ever made it to the *boyfriend* category.

Despite all that she had, Sade knew and felt that her life was missing something. There was no one to spill the beans to at night, to fight with for the remote control, or to argue with about leaving the toilet seat up. "Lord, please send me someone, because all the men I have don't amount to anything," she prayed. There was Donavan, a smooth talker from Brooklyn who spoke with a fake Texas accent. There was also Mikey, a carpenter from down south who only called when he was in the "cittee". Then there was Richard, a wealthy Jamaican businessman who would take her to Red Lobster, only on $9.99 shrimp days. He always insisted that she should only have the shrimp, as he did not think that she could eat anymore than that. "What a cheapskate," she thought. All of these men amounted to nothing at the end of the day.

Even with all of Sade's "prospects", she still felt lonely, knowing that none made her feel that special spark inside, that certain giddy feeling in the pit of her stomach. "What sense does it make?" she wondered. "Why bother to be with someone just for the sake of being with someone? Maybe I should break it off with all these guys, and just wait for the right one to come by. But then what am I going to do on a Saturday night?"

*Chapter #5*_____

Don't:

If you call him once and the call is not returned, take three days at least to return his call when he does. Twitter, MySpace, or Facebook should be his desperate move to get in touch with you. Don't you ever dare chase after any man!

Okay, so you have had a great date, he seems like a wonderful man and you think that he is "the one". You can see him as the father of your future children and the love of your life. You go home and are all gushy and in love, and you call him and tell him in your sweetest voice, "what a wonderful time you had." Only problem though, is that he never calls you back and does not even send you a text or an e-mail. With technology these days, there is just no excuse. If he has not called or "Facebooked" you, get the point my friend; he is not that interested.

Women tend to try to *force* the issue with a man. Okay, so you like him a lot and you have already picked out your bridesmaid dresses and your drapes for your house in the suburbs. Unfortunately, he has not! So you "will" yourself (and him, too), to let this dream of yours come true. But he has not even called once to at least begin the actual baby-making and family-building process. You don't need a crystal ball or a psychologist to tell you what is going on. Men are very simple creatures, and if they like you, they will find you, no matter where in the world you are. Your job is not to make it easier for him by picking up the phone and calling him constantly, like the stalker girlfriend of his nightmares. You do not have to tell him "what a great time you had" and "when are you two going to get together again?" That is the last thing you should do, even if you want to desperately.

So let's just say that you did not get this book in time and you did the unthinkable and called him after your date. Since we cannot go back, let's move forward. You never, ever call him back again until at least three days after your first wrong move—even if he has called you. The one thing that *you* are not is "desperate". Not because you are trying not to seem desperate, but because you really are not. The difference between you and the other women, who are constantly trying to win his attention, is that you don't need him to succeed and to thrive.

There is no pretense in this statement, as the only things that should be on your mind are your career, your family, and your well-being. Finding the right man is like finding the right shoe; they are all so pretty and shiny, but they don't all fit! Your man should fit into your world, not you into his. From my experience with men (and there have been a few), I have surmised that men will take and take and take, until you have no more to give. You have to put your foot down from the very beginning if you want your prospective man to know that you are not at his beck and call.

You do this by **not** making yourself available for him whenever he wants, and by not calling him constantly, as if your day depended upon his voice. Men pick up on desperation, so don't act like a desperate chick! *He* should be working overtime to get to you and wondering where *you* are, not the other way around. It is common knowledge that there are more women out there than men, so make sure that he knows that he has an independent woman who can stand on her own two feet if need be. You do not need a man, you might want one, but you don't *need* one.

Sandy Daley

"Give a man a free hand and he'll run it all over you."

-MAE WEST

HELEN

"If women didn't exist, all the money in the world would have no meaning."

-Aristotle Onassis

The woman with no time for herself. The sistah from Chi town! Isn't that Oprah's stomping ground?

Okay, so Helen was not the sexiest of women, but she wasn't the dowdiest either. With a pretty smile, a nice figure, and a somewhat average look, she could still turn a few heads. Not every man's head, of course, but she was still somewhat attractive. Being the single mother of two boys, age seven and five, was certainly tiring, although she loved every minute of motherhood. Her children were her world; yet she wished that she had more time to herself and, of course, more money in her pocket.

When Terrence, her previous husband and the father of her two children, left three years ago, she thought it would be all fine. "I can raise these boys by myself," she thought. "I mean, it's not like Terrence was doing so much," she reasoned. "I mean, if he was the only one bringing in the dough, maybe I would be more inclined to stay with him after I found out that he was cheating with that exotic dancer down on Main Street." Unfortunately for her, it was never that easy after Terrence left.

She was in charge of everything in the household, including the bills and the children. Terrence not only reneged on his duties as a husband, but as a father as well. He had missed a few months of child support money because he "just didn't have it to give."

With such a burden to carry and not many people to lean on for support, Helen, at thirty-three years of age, began to look more like forty. "Maybe I should have stayed with Terrence," she thought. "I mean, he was not so bad after all, right, Jenny?" she confided to her girlfriend Jenny. Maybe I pushed him to cheat on me." "It is not your fault," said Jenny, trying to console her. "The guy was a jerk. Look, he does not even pay you child support on time. What does that tell you about him?" she asked.

'Jenny is right," Helen thought. "I just have to push through these hard times and it will get better. The kids will grow up and they will find their way. Maybe then I can go back to school and finish the degree that I started."

"Gosh, I will be almost fifty then," she laughed to herself.

Sandy Daley

"A woman without a man is like a fish without a bicycle."

-GLORIA STEINEM

*Chapter #6*_____

Do:

He breaks it; he buys it (marriage or a very good child support payment each month)

So you have made a mistake: you did not use a condom or birth control and have found yourself pregnant, and you are single. It is *your* decision and God's to decide if you are able to take care of this child on your own. I will not, and cannot help you on this matter to decide. Let's just say that you have decided to be strong -good for you- and the little bundle of joy that is in your stomach will be here soon. You have to buck up and become a responsible human being and mother.

If your Baby Daddy (for the lack of a better word), will marry you, and you either love him or can grow to love him, go for it. Marry the schmuck! The only reasons that you should not, is if either you are being physically or verbally abused, or if he has no ambitions to succeed. As a single mother, believe me when I tell you that without any help, you will suffer in many ways. You will give up opportunities -rightfully so, of course, as you are the parent- to ensure that you take care of your bundle of joy. Your child will need so much from you and you will have to provide, one way or another. And let's not talk about the teenage or College years! You might as well resign yourself to working overtime constantly, having ten jobs, plus no love or sex life. So why do it alone if you don't have to? Most of the work will be on you. If your prospective Baby Daddy is a responsible man and has decided to step up to the plate to be a husband and father, let him.

On the other hand, suppose he does not wish to be responsible, but you have his address and all the other information to *force him* to step up to the plate and help out financially? I know that perhaps going to the courts may not be a welcome idea, but don't be one of those women who say, "I am an independent woman I can do this on my own." We are not denying that you are independent and can do this on your own, but you did not get pregnant on your own, did you? Cut the crap and take him to the court office and get the support that your child needs. If you can work out a settlement each month and it is reliable and comes when it is supposed to, then stick with it. Why involve the government in your business if you don't have to? Some men are good this way, and realize that children are a responsibility. Those men financially and emotionally support their children; even if they do not live with them.

But *once*, and if ever, that arrangement begins to slip and you are searching for him or making calls that are not being returned, or you are being insulted by him or his new "baby mama", take the high road and go for child support. You will have a much better relationship if money is not being argued about every month. This gives you both an opportunity to focus on being good parents, and maybe even friends. Your child needs the money, and supportive parents, and you need the help; so take it! Don't be a, "I can do this all by myself girl." Maybe you can, but life will not be an easy road.

Sandy Daley

"Men are so willing to respect anything that bores them."
-Marilyn Monroe

JOSEPHINE

"When I have one foot in the grave, I will tell the whole truth about women. I shall tell it, jump into my coffin, pull the lid over me and say, 'Do what you like now'."

-Leo Tolstoy

Good Hair-all the time: sex-sometimes. The Brooklyn native! Once you have a BK woman, you need nothing else! They are your real ride or die chicks!

Josephine was a very sexy lady and she knew it. Her breasts, a size 36C- the result of a wonderful boob, bounced from side to side in unison. Her hair or weave (whichever you wished to call it), bounced along with her breasts as she walked; with purpose. It is 9:45am and she is late for her 9:50am appointment. If she gets there a minute late, she knows that she is likely to lose her spot.

Her hairdresser is one of the most sought after stylists in the city, and Josephine does not have the patience to deal with all the other patrons today! She has to get to work by 1pm, and that is even pushing it, as she really needs to be there earlier.

She hurries along the side streets, almost tempted to take off her stilettos and run. "If only it was not broad daylight," she thinks to herself. As she scurries along the road, she clutches her knock-off Prada handbag, holding on tight for dear life. "Don't want to get robbed here," she thought. "These people here in this part of the city have no damn conscience and love to take what does not belong to them."She thinks about the contents of her purse, trying to remember if she had picked up her Remy Hair off the night-stand where she had placed it. Eighteen inches and all of fine human hair, mixed with black and the tiniest hint of brown to add color and texture. She peers into her bag, all the while making sure to check out of the corner of her eye for anyone wishing to rob her. "Yes!" she screamed. She had remembered to pick up the hair off the stand. "Whew, what a scare that was," she thought to herself. "I would have had to go back home and for sure I would have been late."

Hair was extremely important to Josephine, as it had been instilled in her to "get your hair taken care of properly," by her mother when she was a little girl. Not only was it expensive to buy-$200 a pack- and she always bought two packs at least to get her hair done over. The significance of beautiful long flowing hair enabled her to fit in, to move up on the success ladder in the corporate world.

Her job as an accountant in Manhattan was a great one, and she knew that her almost Caucasian style of weave helped her achieve certain success. Just as long as she knew that she was still a "sistah", it did not matter to her what people thought. As long as she knew how to act accordingly when she was at black events, versus white events, was all that mattered to her.

The only problem though was which man was she ever going to find that understood her need for $200 hair every month? Not many she reckoned. Maybe that had something to do with her being single at 35? Was she too high maintenance? Too much to handle? Unless she found a rich man of course! A baller, a player whose only concern was to make sure that his woman looked great while walking with him. "Yes, that is it! I'll become a trophy wife," she thought jokingly, as she pushed the salon door open! Damn, there was that bitch Fiona sitting in the styling chair, eating her bagel with cream cheese very slowly, in her tight leotards! "How does that girl get here so early?" Josephine asked herself. "Does she sleep here overnight? I mean seriously, this girl must have a sleeping bag tucked away somewhere in the back because this is ridiculous," Josephine fumed under her breath as she sat down in a vacant seat. "I might have to break her legs one of these days," she laughed to herself, trying to find the humor in the situation.

*Chapter #7*_____

Don't:

No coochie before the lootie (make sure that he spends lots of money on you before you sleep with him. (Consider yourself much more expensive than a Bentley or a Bugatti. You are priceless baby)!

Have you ever noticed the relationship that men have with money? How much they value the dollars in their pockets and what it allows them to buy? Notice the way they drive off in the fast, new Mercedes or Jeep, making sure that it is squeaky clean, and that nothing messes up their pretty little rims? Have you ever seen the look on their faces when you accidentally scratch their favorite vinyl or *slam* their car doors supposedly *too hard*? The point of all of this is that men only understand and try to hold onto things of value. Now, each person has their own sense of value, and he might not see you as something to value. However, it really and truly does not matter if he values you. You have to place the value on yourself.

Now let's say that the guy that you like has shown some interest. Think of yourself as an expensive car! Before you even let him get a sniff or taste, whichever is your fancy, of the juicy center between your legs, make sure that he knows what he is really getting. I know, the thought of making love to your sexy new dude is overwhelming, but you must show restraint. You know the saying that your mother or older girlfriends told you that you should "make him work for it"? Go one step further and make it him pay for it! In other words, show your *real* worth.

We all know that women's liberation has changed a lot for us ladies, but one thing will never change — and although there are a lot of good things that have transpired since those days — is that men love a chase. If they have to work hard for you, they somehow see you as being of value. They now have a stake in you; in *their* minds of course. Please remember however, that he does not own you and has no claim whatsoever on you, so if ever you wish to leave the relationship, for whatever reason, then leave.

However, let him continue to be the man that he should be, by paying for the things that he needs to. If you go out to dinner the first few times, don't you dare come out of your pocket or go Dutch. If he cannot afford to take you to a nice restaurant the first few times on *his* dime, then sit your happy little single butt at home and read a book! Going to McDonald's or Taco Bell should *not* be okay for you on your first few dates. If he ever becomes your *boyfriend* in the future, that however is a different situation.

A man's job is to be a man, and to show you why *you* should even think about being with him. If he cannot afford to take you out to that nice restaurant on those first few dates, if it means anything to him, he will work as hard as he can in order to take you out. Working overtime at his job is not an issue. Now, he should not steal for you, but he should feel as if he has lost a lot if he does not have you. His happy little behind will do anything, apart from stealing, to be able to afford the girl of his dreams — you. We all know that you can take care of yourself, but that is not the point here.

The point is that if *he* wants you, *he* needs to work hard to get and keep you. Don't let him off the hook by lowering your standards by feeling sorry for him. He needs to earn you and care for you, just like he does his shiny new Mercedes or Bugatti, with the brand new rims!

"Nearly all men can stand adversity, but if you want to test a man's character, give him power."

-ABRAHAM LINCOLN

RHONDA_____

"Some women hold up dresses that are so ugly and they always say the same thing: 'This looks much better on.' On what? On fire?"

-Rita Rudner

"Whose Vagina Is It, Really?"- How much crap was she going to believe? I need to sell her a pig farm in the sky! The Georgia Peach: Atlanta, Georgia that is!

It was safe to say that Rhonda was in love with Daniel; with his swagger, his smooth words, his masculine build and his ability to make her feel sexy. She has been dating Daniel for over five months. She knew that she was not the only girl that he was seeing, but still hangs on to the hope that he will commit to her fully one day. She makes love to him whenever he wants, does whatever he says; even if she is against it.

He seldom returns her calls, never has enough money for dates, and demands that she be faithful to him, even though he gives nothing back in return. While in bed, he constantly tells her that her vagina belongs to him, even though he makes it clear that she is not his only "female", as he calls women.

"Why do you stay with the guy?" her friend Marcia enquired. "It is not like you can't get another man. You are good looking, funny and sexy! Break it off with him and find yourself a guy who is going to deal with you, and only you. So what if he says that your vagina is his? That means nothing in the grand scheme of things."

Rhonda knew that Marcia was right! Why can't she break up with him? It's not like he tells her he loves her or wants a future with her. Staking claim on her vagina does not mean that he wants a future with her! Still, she stays, clinging on to the hope that he will make her his woman someday. Sex was so good with Daniel! How could she let another woman have that?

*Chapter #8*_____

Do:

When your man or ex-man decides to ask you, "Whose is it, baby?" -And you know they all do-look him straight in the eye and tell him that it is his! Lie, lie, and lie, like a hooker telling her "John" that she "usually, does not do this, and so it is going to cost him more!"

Like you, I have never had a lover or a boyfriend who hasn't asked me this question. Most times, of course, it is in bed during a fantastic lovemaking session, but often times it is asked even months after a break-up. Needless to say, I, perhaps like you, would answer with the utmost of pride, excitement and glee. Your goal of course, to please and urge your man on, in order for him to perform better. However, have you ever asked yourself, why does your man wish to know if your God-given private parts belong to him and him only?

What do you say to that same man when he asks you that same question even after a break-up? What is the correct response? Should you then turn allow them to stake same claim on your private parts? *Can* you?

Men will ask you that question for one simple reason; control. It really has nothing to do with their love for you. In their minds, once they have control of your vagina (the most important body part that other men will desire from you as well), they have become a conqueror — *the one who conquered that vagina.* Unfortunately, even after breaking up, they believe your vagina — not you, but the vagina they fought so hard to get — belongs to no other. So, this is what you do to figure out what your Mr. Wonderful *really* wants from you. Whenever he asks you that question, do not be offended and turned off by his crassness, but remember where this question is coming from.

His need to be the conqueror of his domain, permeates through his veins and there is nothing that you can do about it. Anytime that a man asks you ,"Is it mine baby?" answer him in the sexiest voice that you can, no matter where you are, "Yours, baby! You know that it belongs to you and only you. Unfortunately, I cannot concentrate on you right now as the phone company is threatening to cut off my phone for non-payment and I am just a little worried right now. I just have to deal with this issue!"

Now, this may seem like such a game to you and very deceitful, but there is a method to this madness, as they say. If his first response to you is, "Sorry to hear that, and I wish that I could help you with your problems," then you know that he is not the right man for you.

However, if he says to you, "Crap! How much do you owe and when do you have to pay it by?" Or even, "How much of it do you have already?", then you know that he is worth giving a chance. You really do not want anything from him, and you should not accept it if he offers (if you are not his girlfriend already), but you are just testing him. His answer will tell you many things about his true intentions for you.

Either answer tells you exactly what he has in his mind. If he cares about you at all, not only your vagina, your problems should be of his concern. If he doesn't feel sorry for your plight and just wishes to talk to you during good times, run far away from him. If he is worth keeping, it should not matter to him whether or not you sleep with him. He should not be trying to control you with money, or things in order to keep you. Use the power of your vagina to get to know who you are really dealing with.

If you play your cards right, you don't ever have to give yourself to someone who does not deserve you. I play this trick all the time, as it tells me very quickly what category to put a guy in. The objective here is to save yourself time, and lots of heartache in the long run. If a man really wants to stick around, there is nothing that he will not do for you. Test him and you will get the answers that you need.

*Desiree*_____

"My wife is the sort of woman who gives necrophilia a bad name."

-Patrick Murray

No more Granny Panties Please!

The mulatto living in San Francisco. How much china do you really need?

Michael and Desiree's marriage was, at best, a troubled one, filled with arguments, fuss and strife. They had married young, high on the expectations of a wonderful future. But somewhere along the line they lost it. Both became pre-occupied with work, and only communicated when necessary. Gone were the days when Desiree would dress up in her sexy red teddy, heels on her feet and jewels around her neck, to bed. Gone were the days of red wine at dinner, followed by passionate lovemaking on the kitchen table, or on the floor.

Now, Desiree had no desire to wear a sexy thong and garter belts. Instead she opted for sweat pants, head tie and a mud mask to bed. It wasn't like Michael was in the bedroom anymore anyways! She couldn't even remember the last time they'd had sex or had been intimate. It was like they'd both stopped caring. Was Michael cheating on her? Was he making advances to other women, her friends perhaps? It couldn't hurt to get dressed up like she used to. But after thinking about the mortgage, and looking after the kids all day, she just didn't have the time or energy. Looking good was secondary, getting enough sleep was primary.

Desiree confessed these thoughts to her friend June. "June, I don't know what to do anymore," she said. I just don't care about dressing sexy at all these days." "Now is the time that you should try to look your best. You have no idea who might be after your husband," said June, thinking about Michael in his tight tennis pants the last time that she seen him while visiting Desiree. He was a good looking man, who had made passes at her more than once. She had however never mentioned this to Desiree.

"Some women just do not appreciate what they have at home," said June to herself.

*Chapter #9*_____

Do:

Dress like the sex-pot that you are. For God's sake no sweat pants, face-cream, and mouth-guard to bed. Get a stripper pole in the bedroom if you want to! Men want a lady in the streets and a whore in the bedroom!

Do you own a pair of jogging pants or even sweatshirts? If you said yes, please tell me *why*? If you do, these items should only be worn while doing laundry and taken off once you are finished. Unless of course, they are sexy jogging pants with "sexy hot mama" engraved on the backside. Looking good should never be a chore. Try to always look great and be the total diva, not only for others, but for yourself. When we look and feel good we walk with confidence, we have a distinct and purposeful stride to our walk. Also, remember that men are visual creatures.

Have you ever walked the streets with your man, husband, son or even father, and seen them stare at other women? Even though they try to hide the fact that they are looking. It does not necessarily mean that they want to bang that other woman; it is just that they are visual creatures. Use this knowledge to your advantage.

Go to the gym often or enroll in a yoga class. Gyms are open from early morning till late night, or even twenty-four hours. In other words, there is no excuse for you not to take care of yourself. Put makeup on. If you don't know how, take a class somewhere to get the best information about makeup. Buy nice clothes for yourself, even if you have children. The more time that you spend on yourself, the more others will appreciate you.

Unfortunately, after a few years of marriage some women seem to let themselves go. Many act on the premise of "So I already have my man, why do I need to look sexy?" Do you remember when he first met you, what you looked like? Remember, you are still not doing this for someone else but for your own self-esteem. Your goal here is to always enhance your own God-given talents in pursuit of your own happiness. God gave this body to you to keep, right? Use it wisely. Often, once we get married we let ourselves go so much that we become unrecognizable to our husbands and partners.

We are no longer the girl that they want to spend their lives with, much less a bed and a home. This, in a man's eyes is seen as being deceitful, as men are left thinking, "Where is that girl that I asked to be my wife and who is this sweats-wearing, roller-curlers, no-make-up woman in my bed?" They married you for a reason; because they liked who you were when they first started talking to you. Don't emotionally and physically disappoint yourself and your man while you are in the relationship.

It seems like common sense, but you must really examine this situation to finally understand. Your health, physical appearance, and overall well-being should be important to you, even while you age. Isn't it a form of emotional cheating when you detach yourself from your own spirits and also your husband's?

Sandy Daley

"Within the covers of the Bible are the answers for all the problems men face."

-RONALD REAGAN

Nicky

"No man knows more about women than I do, and I know nothing."

-Seymour Hicks

The E-Harmony and Match.com girl. The Sexy Torontonian: Oh Canada eh? I wonder if she lives in an igloo.

Nicky was very excited. She had met her Mr. Wonderful recently on one of the more popular internet dating sites, and she told everyone. He was tall, dark and handsome, and spoke with a quiet confidence. He was the type of man that all her girlfriends would love. He was also intelligent, funny and articulate, and he made her legs buckle under her when they spoke on the phone. And he was great in bed as well. Hung like a horse, is what she told her girlfriends; how could she have gotten so lucky? The only problem is that she noticed, much to her chagrin that he was still on the dating site, even months after they were now supposedly dating "exclusively".

When asked about it, his answer was that he had paid for a whole year's worth of membership. Although he had met the girl of his dreams -her of course- his membership could not be cancelled. He was on the site still as a *courtesy*, and could not come off voluntarily. He assured her not to worry, as he loved her, and had certainly gotten a great return on his investment.

"Stop worrying Nicky and stop acting so insecure," he said to her. "So what if I am on a dating site; that is how we met right? Are you turning your nose now up at dating sites?" "No," she replied to him. "But I cannot understand why you cannot just cancel your membership if we are seeing each other exclusively. Why do you still have to be on there?" For months this went on, and low and behold, what did Nicky find out a few months later? That her Mr. Wonderful was not only on this *one* particular site, but while doing a little bit of investigating (okay, so she had jumped into his email, by accident of course, while on a visit to his home) was on other sites as well. Her Mr. Wonderful was also dating at least five other women from other dating sites as well. He also had the same user name! What a fool she was, she thought, and how dumb of him to use the same name. "Geez," she thought. "No creativity!"

*Chapter #10*_____

Don't:

Internet dating? Only if you are very ugly and want to hide behind a computer! Do you know how many married men pretend to be single, and have different usernames on many different dating sites?

So the Internet rules our lives and we can now buy everything online, from clothes, to shoes to groceries to pharmaceuticals- and everything in between. The Internet has fooled us into thinking that everything that comes from there is good and can be trusted. No one even buys a newspaper anymore, as everyone turns to the Internet as their trusted source for news and information.

Unfortunately, with the explosion of the Internet and all that comes with it, dating sites have popped up all over the place, with each site making it easier for you to find your Mr. Right or Mr. Right Now, (whichever one suits your fancy). From sites such as eHarmony to

Match.com, your love is just around the corner. All you have to do is log on, pay a small monthly fee, and your Mr. Wonderful will appear, on a white horse, with good credit, no kids and pearly white teeth.

Girl, don't be stupid! I have personally fallen prey to this conundrum (which incidentally is one of the reason why I began writing *Whose Vagina Is It, Really?*) At least I can thank that jerk for being himself, but I am at fault as well for believing the hype. Unless you are a writer, however, and can gain from the Internet dating mistake, the only thing that will happen is money and time lost by you, and you feeling used at the end of the ordeal. Not only would you have been duped by men in your own hometown, but by men from across the seas as well. Oh, that horrible sinking feeling!

The one thing that your Mr. Wonderful might not be telling you is that, while he is on one site as "Hunglikeastud" saying such things as, "Good Morning Baby, I see you posted a new picture showing all your twins- Wow what size are they?", he is also signed under username, "Yourwaitinghusband", who is seeking a wife who will love him and his cute little Labrador. His messages to you then are, "When you become my woman, I will want new pictures from you, again, I don't want to share you." He could also be saying to you, "I love your playful nature, so let's play. You don't recognize your man when you see him?" He might be on all of the dating sites without your knowledge of course, while you run around telling all your girlfriends that you have met your "husband" finally. Nonetheless, the Internet is a place for quick fixes, impromptu purchases, and must-have items.

Do you really believe that finding the partner for such a diva such as yourself should be left to a source where diapers and dog food are sold, and where porn is the biggest source of entertainment? Why leave your happiness to such an untrustworthy tool as the internet? It is so clouded with so much information it cannot possibly get your wishes right. Can you really believe the photo in front of you on your computer screen is really who you are speaking to? With the quick change of a photo, your "Mr. Hot stuff" could really be a nerd with big teeth, an overbite, and hair coming out of his ears and nose, and no hair. Of course we are not saying that looks is everything, but it does account for something in a relationship.

You should feel attracted to your partner, not only intellectually, but also physically as well. Married men, and also men *supposedly* in a committed relationship, often use the Internet to cheat on their partners. Unless you signed up for this willingly and have signed up with Ashley Madison-the cheating dating site- why be a part of a hurtful situation unknowingly? In a nutshell, not even if you look like one of the witches from the Macbeth story, should you even consider dating someone on the Internet. It rarely works out. Your Mr.

Right—the same Mr. Right Now, under many different usernames and on different sites-will certainly just be a waste of time and money.

Brenda

As Miss America, my goal is to bring peace to the entire world and then get my own apartment."

-Jay Leno

The Gym rat! From Arkansas: I wonder if Hilary and Bill Clinton still have a home there? I wonder if Monica Lewinsky has ever visited?

Brenda could not remember the last time that she had a date, or even talked on the phone at length with a man. She could not remember the last time she held hands with a broad-shouldered man or kissed anyone under the sunset. Her love life was sparse, none existent, and oh so lonely.

She was not bad to look at though; her nicely rounded rear, sculpted perfectly from years spent in the gym daily, was always greatly admired. Her daily routine, come hell or high water, rain or shine, was the most fixed and concrete thing in her life. At twenty-eight and unmarried with no prospects in sight, her consolation prize of a perfect body seemed almost within her grasp as she sweated profusely in her cycling class daily.

The only person that made her smile these days was her friend Tony. He was kind, friendly, sexy, and a really nice guy. But he was also married, with children. He had started sending Brenda flowers, giving her car rides, and even offered to help her out with a few of her bills. Now, she knew this was wrong — but really and truly, what was so wrong about being "friendly" with him? Tony was a nice guy to her and she needed a friend; someone to talk to.

Her friends could not understand her logic as they often interrogated her about her choice to spend every living moment in the gym, and not out dating or looking for a man, other than Tony. "Girl, what is wrong with you?" they would ask. "Don't you see that you are getting older and there is not even a boyfriend in sight? Is that how you want to live Brenda? What are you running away from?" To these questions, Brenda had no answer, as she would often wonder the same things herself.

What was her problem? What was she really scared of? Love? Was spinning and weights more manageable than a man with real feelings and a flesh? To these questions she had no concrete answer. Tony was a good choice for now, as even though she really did like him a lot, he was not interrupting her life.

She hoped that someday she would summon up the courage to leave her escapism behind her, and really plunge into an adult relationship, where anything was possible. Even everlasting love! For now however, she was content on being the first to finish her ride on the bike, and the first to wipe her sweat from her forehead. The cycling instructor always commented that she was "wonderful and magnetic to watch on the bike." She smiled and said to herself, "Geez, the instructor was not so bad looking." Maybe just maybe there would be a love connection at the gym after all.

But really, why bother screw up a good thing? For now, Tony was her escape, even though the relationship was going nowhere.

Sandy Daley

"All men are prepared to accomplish the incredible if their ideals are threatened."
-MAYA ANGELOU

*Chapter #11*_____

Do:

Stay away from married men! He will never leave his wife for you no matter what he says. By the time he does you will have an old, grey, shriveled vagina, and he no longer wants you

Never date a married man! Why would you want to anyway? You will never be seen as number one -which you are. Also if your affair is ever discovered, he will deny you in a heartbeat. Men who cheat really have no intentions of ever leaving their wives. The only reason why they are with you is to get something that their wife is not giving to them. His wife has now stopped wearing the sexy lingerie and stilettos to bed, and is now in track pants and rollers; no longer trying to appear sexy to her man.

Now, the only thing left for him to do is to find himself a little honey on the side, who will continue to fulfill his sexual desires without costing him too much. You, of course, are the schmuck that he has set his eyes on to fill that void. He keeps swearing to you that he "is definitely going to divorce her and then marry you!" How many affairs ever turn into marriages? You will waste all your life waiting for your Mr. Wonderful to divorce his wife, while your vagina hairs get greyer and greyer from old age.

The other thing to consider is that, most times when men do leave their wives and go their separate ways, they *rarely* get into a relationship with the woman that they were having the affair with. They feel that they are now finally free and can bang as many young chicks — excluding you with the grey vagina hairs — that they can.

So what would have been the outcome? You would have wasted all your Saturday nights and holidays, longing for your Mr. Wonderful to be by your side, wishing he was holding you in his arms. He is able to sneak a call here and there, when his wife, who usually is the boss of him, bellows in the background for him to "come and take out the garbage". In your mind you are thinking, "How could he ever continue to be with her, while I am available with my sexy body and supportive character? Does he not know that I love him?"

Get a grip girl! The only reason he continues to be with her is because he *loves* her. This is quite evident because he is still by her side, even with her nasty attitude, sweatpants, and rollers in her hair. The communication in his marriage might have just broken down and he needs a shoulder a cry on and someone to talk to. Don't be the schmuck and the mistress on the side. It should be very obvious to you that he really cares for his wife, because not only is she not doing the right things to keep her man but you *are* doing the right things, aren't you? And who is he married you? Her, not you!

And if ever your *affair* is discovered, he will fabricate every excuse in the book, and even go as far as call you a *liar* when he is caught. He might even go as far as saying that he is a "sex addict", which is the most common cop-out these days for men, and some women, when they are caught cheating.

There is nothing wrong with being friends with a married man, but do remember that there are lines to draw between your friendships. If you find it getting too *cozy*, or if you are starting to feel attracted to him - which is not a wrong emotion- distance yourself immediately. Being attracted to someone is not wrong, but acting upon the emotion is morally wrong. Unless you are prepared to waste your life on something that will never be yours, dating a married man should never be an option. Besides, why would you ever want to be second to any other woman? There are lots of men out there so go out and get your own!

"Between men and women there is no friendship possible.
There is passion, enmity, worship, love, but no friendship."

-OSCAR WILDE

Michelle

"When a woman becomes a scholar there is usually
something wrong with her sexual organs."

-Friedrich Nietzsche

*The Choosey One! Manhattan girl: "If you can make
it here, you can make it anywhere"!*

She walks with confidence. Her job as a stock broker in
Manhattan is secure, with benefits and a great stock
portfolio to match. Her apartment is filled with the
nicest of things, art décor and furniture that you would
die for. She vacations in the South of France, with
wealthy friends with manicured dogs and pricey jewels.
Yet, she is not happy because there is no man by her
side. In the business-world, Michelle is a success, with
a six-figure salary and a high rise apartment.

At Thirty-five, her biological clock is ticking fast and her
dreams of being a wife to a good man seem to be fading
in the dark, as the days go by without a wedding ring
on her finger. Being a success in the business world is
not enough for her mother who looks at her, with all her
accomplishments as somewhat of a failure. "When are
you going to find a husband Michelle?" her mother asks

101

her over and over again. "Why are you so picky, so difficult? What exactly are you looking for in a husband? You are going to continue being so picky that you will end up with no one. Find a man and learn to love him! What good is your money if there is no-one to love you while you have it? It is your fault for not having a man!" Michelle smiled to herself and replied, inwardly of course, "I do know what I want. He has just not appeared as yet."

*Chapter #12*_____

Don't

Why marry for money when you can make your own? The last thing that you want is a man to control you! Put yourself in a position to say, "Piss off and I really don't care how much money you have or what you drive. You can't buy my love or affection!" to a man at any time

Money does rule the world and often times money is used to control you, make you feel less than. Money dictates the quality of life that you live, and without money you cannot survive.

Unfortunately, a lot of times we make less money - even though we might do the same quality, and quantity of work as a man in the workforce. This then leads you to perhaps marry for stability to ensure that you will live comfortable. Money does not make you happy, so don't ever throw in the towel and settle with a man just because he is financially stable. Great if you find, and love someone who is wealthy and you two have decided to make a life together. However, succumbing to fear and marrying for money while you stare at your dwindling bank account is not the answer.

Have you ever seen those wealthy women, driving around in Bentleys, with Gucci handbags, butler and all, who no matter how much money they may have, they are not happy? They may often turn to the bottle, drugs, infidelity and worse, just to fill a void. Do you think that it is just boredom why they act out in such ways? No, it is not! It is their inner voices telling them that they perhaps do *not* deserve what they have, and have not worked for it. There was no sweat or tears poured over their material things, so losing it or even jeopardizing their lifestyle is nothing to them. They did not work for it.

However, do you ever see the middle class or financially challenged woman, perhaps with kids in tow and a husband who works from dusk till dawn, how protective she is of her family? *She* knows the blood, sweat and tears that it took for her to acquire what she has. The other thing to consider is that, with your own money, you will have the control of your own life. You will not be left prey to men who wish to only use you for sexual pleasures. They are less likely to treat you with disrespect, as you are seen as their equal, someone to be reckoned with.

Even if you are a married woman, find something that allows you to be financially independent. You never know what might happen in the future, right? With this extra income, you will walk faster, stand more proudly and be more independent. You are able to provide for your children on your own, if it ever comes down to that. The amount of women that I have met in the past who depend on their husbands for financial support is staggering and disheartening.

I vividly remember the tears of one beautiful Persian girl, a member at the gym where I worked out, a few years ago. She was told by her husband that she had to quit working out, as he did not see the need for it. She was a stay at home mom, with four children and had no other means of income but her husband's. She had no choice but to quit as he had demanded. I will never forget her eyes the day that she left the gym, never to return. As I watched the tears roll from her eyes, which were bright red and puffy, I vowed never to let that happen to me. "Better to be poor and in control of my own life," I thought to myself as I watched her leave the gym.

Bonus dos and don'ts:

These things must be said. No Case

Studies needed at all!

*Chapter #13*_____

Do:

If he ever hits you: leave him immediately! He will never respect you in any way and will always see you as being weak. Would he ever want someone to bitch slap his mother or his sister? No, of course not, as no woman deserves to be abused!

Now this is one of the most serious topics in this book and must be discussed. Women are abused every single day at an alarming rate. Although of course the blame rests with the abuser, you must also take some of the responsibility if you decide to stay in a verbally, or physically abusive relationship.

The minute that these things begin to happen, it is a sign for you to leave. There should be no thoughts of "what is going to happen to you or the kids if you decide to leave". You will find a way! Even if you have to go to a shelter or stay with family or friends for a time being; somebody will help you. There is no shame in being abused, as the shame is not in your eyes. However, your actions dictate the outcome if you continue to abide in such horrible conditions. Worse if you have children! You should never desire for your kids to see this abuse, as this will impact them greatly during their formative years, and also during adult life.

Boys often act out in the same manner as their fathers. If they see this on a regular basis in their home while developing into adulthood, they are often left emotionally scarred for life. Both boys and girls often have problems developing healthy relationships when they get older. Also, not only will a black eye or scarred shoulders or knees display itself on your body, but emotionally it will rob you of your self esteem. As a young woman, I experienced abuse at the hand of an ex-boyfriend, and it is not something that you easily recover from. I had to re-program myself and *find* myself again. This was not an easy task, and it took me years to recover emotionally.

So, leave immediately if this is happening to you. You will begin to feel less than; and feeling less than is not a good feeling. You will forever doubt yourself and your abilities as a productive human being. Your children will understand and love you no matter what; even while you shack up with your mother for a few years while you *figure* things out. The couch or basement is much better than a hole in the ground, right?

*Chapter # 14*_____

Do:

To threesome or not to threesome (Only if it is your fantasy). The biggest mistake that you can ever make is to bring another woman in your bed at his request. He is not even satisfying you completely in bed but wants another at the same time? The nerve!

So he wants a threesome huh? Now, the one thing that I have discovered with this *desire,* is that it really is not a desire, just a passing, upwardly mobile fancy. You and I both know that he will never be able to please both of you, (even if he takes ten Viagra's at the same time). Someone, more than likely you, will walk away from the experience feeling let down. Also during the experience, he will be thinking, "Damn, I wonder if I should turn to the left or go to the right. Should I nibble here or nibble there?"

His brain will be so caught up in the *technicalities* of the deed, that enjoyment for all parties will seriously be jeopardized and compromised. You will be forever thinking, "Geez, now why did he turn to her most of the times during the act and really and truly how ugly do I look to this strange person in my bed at this moment in time? I wonder if she has a hidden camera somewhere here and the next thing that I am going to see is my naked behind on YouTube?"

When he comes to you with this suggestion, which most men will, as they will all try to test the waters to see how freaky you really are, you quickly answer him without a pause. "Sure honey, now right after we do your fantasy, can we then do mine? You know that I have always wanted to have a threesome, and really and truly I have always liked the look of your friend Mark. Does he still have those bow legs?"

Most normal red-blooded man will vehemently shake their heads in disgust and of course say, "NO!" which is what you really want in the first place anyway. Don't let him off the hook as yet though; he brought you here, so you finish it. Continue to further question his logic and the *real* reason why he is saying no in such a quick manner. I mean, you were ready to say yes to him, weren't you?

He will probably say something such as "that's nasty" as he really lets your suggestion and fantasy requests sink in. You and his boys? How dare you suggest something so evil and vile? Still, don't let him off the hook! "But you wanted me and another girl didn't you? So why can't I have the same thing too? Is your fantasy request more important than mine?" you continue to say. Of course he will say "no, and it just that it is a different thing and you will never understand." His male ego and pride would not allow him to see you in that fashion. To him, you are *his* property and no one else's; even though you should be willing the share him. More than likely he will then put his fantasy wishes in the background, as every time that he desires to say something to you, his first thought would be your awful, supposedly *sick fantasy*. Nip it in the bud quickly and you will have nothing to worry about.

Sex should be an enjoyable experience between two people; an opportunity to get closer to your partner in every way. Too often, I find that women will bend over backwards to please their partners, without thinking of the consequences. Yes, you might go along with this to please your man, but really have you thought about what you are doing to yourself? Do not ever engage in something that you will be embarrassed about in the future. Something that makes you uncomfortable. At end of the day, the only person staring at you in the mirror is you, and so if you don't want to engage in a threesome, don't.

But if you do- go for it. Once again, it should be your choice. His porno watching days obviously needs to be curtailed, as it is giving him too many ideas! Once a week, that is it for him and his porno stash!

*Chapter # 15*_____

Do

Little Penis? Oh crap! Okay, so make him compensate for his shortcomings. He should be doing his tongue massages every morning, noon and night!

Okay, so your Mr. Wonderful has a small penis; nothing that you can do about that right? Wrong! Most men are obsessed with the size of their penis. Their every waking moment is spent looking at the guy next to them while in the public washroom, or in the gym's bathroom, while they change after a long workout. Your man, of course drives you nuts while in bed. "Do you like it baby? Am I the biggest and best you have ever had? Am I hurting you?" Oh brother! Now of course you do not wish to hurt his feelings because you care, right? And most importantly *you* know that size does *no*t matter; but let's not tell them that, and instead use this to your advantage.

So this is what you do! Your job is to skillfully, without hurting your "Mr. Wonderful" emotionally, stroke his ego, but you should also introduce the other sexual act that research says, most *pleases* us women. You mention of course, that although you do find his size "okay" and he means a lot to you, you would however appreciate a little extra loving.

You really should say to him, "Honey you know that size does not matter and I love you for who you are, not your penis size." Psychology and the art of persuasion should be your two most common manipulative tools that you use to get what you want. See how fast he gets on his knees or goes *downtown* in order to please you. Not telling him that he is inadequate will make him feel a little bit inadequate and if he wants to keep you, he will do what you want instinctively.

If he does care about you, and deep down he knows that his penis is smaller than average, he will try to compensate in so many other ways. Either by bringing you flowers more often, helping around house and with the kids on a regular basis, or using his tongue to please you. And don't discourage him either; he should always be trying to please you; that is his job. So let him practice his extracurricular exercises with his tongue or hands. What he does not know -which of course is that size does not matter- will not hurt him, but will only enhance *your* pleasure and of course your relationship.

*Chapter #16*_____

Do:

Love yourself before anyone else; but love him wholeheartedly as well if you have chosen him. No more granny panties for you. And stop the nagging!

The one thing that many women do not like to hear, but which we must discuss, is the issue of excessive talking and explaining — or nagging. There is an obvious difference between men and women. Women like to discuss a topic to death, even if they know that it has been resolved.

I admit, I also suffer from this *deadly* disease that seemingly has no cure. I will beat an argument to death, saying the same things fifty times to a guy. Most men would just like for you to tell them what to do once, and it will get done.

115

There is no need, in their minds, to go on and on about the same point. While doing so, they tune us out, trying to figure out how to talk to you without hearing all the other unnecessary crap that goes along with the conversation. Then they clamp up, zoning out completely. So then what happens? All communication shuts down between both parties, and now no one is talking; and thus the demise of this relationship begins. You stop loving each other and supporting each other as partners should in a relationship. The first thing that you need to do is listen and do not try to make him into something that he is not.

We always seem to think that we are saviors of our guys, and it is our job to make them into something. Wrong! The only people that you are responsible for are your children, as they are the only ones that you may shape and mold as you see fit. And that is even limited, because as time goes on, your children will also desire to leave your nest and find a way for themselves. So leave your man alone and stop the nagging. If you are with him in a relationship and you have decided to stick it out with him, love and support him as both he and you deserve. He is your man, not your child or property!

If he has not "put a ring on it" yet, then you decide your fate. Do you stay or do you go? And last, but not least, do not listen to your all of your girlfriends' advice, because as you and I both know, their lives behind closed doors is not really what it cracks up to be most times. So they might be encouraging you to "Leave him, girl, as he ain't doing nothing for you," and they are still living with a man who is outwardly cheating on them or not taking care of them.

The only person's opinion that should be of major concern to you is your own opinion of yourself. Girlfriends should only be good to rest your head on when you are crying, or to vent to when you need to vent ,or to discuss which guy looked hotter in the soaps that day — not to determine the outcome of your life.

"I do not believe in a fate that falls on men however they act;
but I do believe in a fate that falls on them unless they act."

-BUDDHA

Chapter #17_____

ESPECIALLY FOR MY CARIBBEAN SISTAHS:

KARLENE

To generalize on women is dangerous. To specialize on them is infinitely worse.

- Rudolf Valentino

The Kingstonian baby: The real Yardie gal! - No more Black Americans (Dem different bwoy)

Karlene knew that she looked good. She's a Caribbean sister with the big booty, a nice rack and a sweet Jamaican accent that intrigues not only her Caribbean brothers, but also the Black American men as well. At 29 years old, she's intelligent, sexy, and witty and works as an Insurance broker in Atlanta. She's dated Caribbean men, black Americans and even white men. She is what you would call an *International sistah*!

119

Over the last seven years however, she has primarily been dating black Americans, as her social life and job makes it easy for her to meet these types of men. However, her last intimate encounter with one has made her vow to never date another black American again. They are just too different. "What do you mean they are too different?" her friend Jacqueline asks her. "Aren't they all men?"

"There's a major difference," Karlene replies. If I am ever in a jam, I can call a Jamaican man, whether or not I am his main girl, and he will try to help me with my problem. If that same situation happens and I call a black American man, he will tell me to call him back when I figure it out. I just don't think that they know how to deal with women properly. "I think that slavery, and living in America with the struggles that they have had to deal with as black Americans, has messed them up badly bwoy," she says.

"I just want to find a Caribbean brother that probably has only one woman, if he must, on de side with me. I know that I will still get taken care. If him hav two or three on the side, he will not have enough to go around."

*Chapter #18*_____

"Whose Vagina Is It, Really?"

Are you still wondering?

The question still remains, "Whose Vagina Is It, Really?", and this book really never set out to answer the question for you, but to leave it up to you to answer for yourself. "Whose Is It Really?" God's, your man's, your children's, society's? When have you ever had the opportunity to maintain the control of your own life? He who holds the key to the vagina, maintains the control, remember?

Well, I have decided *not* to take the power from you, as others have done in the past. My personal answer, the answer that is for *me* and me alone is; "Mine of course, but yours to play with if I let you!" You may use that line if you like it, as I think it captures the essence of what I tried to say in this book.

What is your answer? Search within yourself and make up your own mind. Your answer is your own *private* answer. Allow no one, not even myself, tell you how to live your own. Hopefully "Whose Vagina Is It, Really?" has opened your eyes to some things, but most importantly, brought you laughter, empowerment and lots of joy.

This was my *true* intention from the very beginning. Hopefully the women featured in "Whose Vagina Is It, Really?" discover the strength within, and figure out who's life they are *really* living. To Anita, Deidra, Josephine, Marsha, Michelle, Brenda, Nicky, Rhonda, Sade, Helen, Desiree, Karlene, Rhonda, and Courtney-Ann and also to Sandy, I say;

To thine own self be true, and it must follow, as the night the day, thou canst not then be false to any man.
-William Shakespeare

When one door closes, another opens; but we often look so long and so regretfully upon the closed door that we do not see the one which has opened for us.

- ALEXANDER GRAHAM BELL

NAMASTE

SANDY DALEY

Sandy Daley

Proof

Made in the USA
Charleston, SC
21 September 2010